A *Sweet*
FRIENDSHIP REFRESHES
THE SOUL

PROVERBS 27:9

This journal Belongs to:

Thank you for your purchase!
Please consider leaving a review. We'd love to hear your honest feedback.

DATE ---------------------------------

DATE

DATE ....

DATE ....

DATE

DATE

DATE ·····························

DATE ....

DATE ----------------------

DATE

DATE

DATE ----------------------------

DATE ----------------------------------

DATE _____

DATE ----------------------------------

DATE

DATE ------------------------------

DATE ----------------------------------

DATE

DATE ----------------------------

DATE --------------------------------

DATE ....

DATE ....

DATE ----------------------------

DATE ----------------------

DATE

DATE

DATE

DATE ----------------------------------

DATE

DATE ....

DATE

DATE ----------------------------------

DATE ....

DATE ----------------------------

DATE ....

DATE

DATE

DATE

DATE ....

DATE

DATE ----------------------------

DATE ....

DATE ....

DATE

DATE --

DATE _____

DATE

DATE --

DATE

DATE

DATE

DATE

DATE

DATE

DATE

DATE

DATE ....

DATE ----------------------------------

DATE

DATE

DATE ....

DATE

DATE ----------------------------

DATE

DATE --

DATE

DATE ----------------------------

DATE

DATE --------------------------

DATE --

DATE ....

DATE ----------------------------

DATE

DATE ....

DATE

DATE

DATE ....

DATE ------------------------------

DATE

DATE ----------------------------------

DATE ----------------------------

DATE

DATE ....

DATE ....

DATE

DATE

DATE

DATE

DATE ....

DATE

DATE ....

DATE ....

DATE ----------------------

DATE ---------------------------

DATE

DATE ----------------------------

DATE ....

DATE _____

DATE ....

DATE ----------------------------

DATE

DATE

DATE

DATE

DATE

DATE

DATE

Made in United States
Orlando, FL
14 October 2022

23400667R00067